Knowledge is Wealth
and
Other Stories

Translated by

Matina Wali Muhammad

Ta-Ha Publishers Ltd.
www.taha.co.uk

Copyright © Ta-Ha Publishers Ltd 1416H/ 1996CE

Reprinted 1998, 2000, 2002

1425AH/October 2004

Published by:
Ta-Ha Publishers Ltd.
1 Wynne Road
London SW9 0BB

Website: http://www.taha.co.uk/
Email: sales@taha.co.uk

Translated by: Matina Wali Muhammad
Edited by: Abdassamad Clarke
Illustrated by: M. Ishaq

A catalogue record of this book is available from the British Library.

ISBN 1 897940 42 4

Printed and Bound in England by: De-Luxe Printers Ltd.

Contents

The Prophet ﷺ and Children

The Prophet ﷺ dearly loved little children. He would always care for them. Whenever he would go out on foot and meet little children, he would wish them well and answer their greetings. Then he would pat them on their heads with affection. Sometimes he would pick them up in his arms. If there were any orphans among them he would try his best to comfort and console them. He would often guide Muslims to take special care of orphans. He said that we should look after orphans as we look after our own children.

Once, there were some people who were dying and they wanted to leave a lot of their property to the poor. That meant that their children would have less money to look after themselves. The Prophet ﷺ would draw the attention of these dying people towards their children. He said we should look after our families. The Prophet ﷺ said, "It is better to leave your relatives well off, instead of leaving nothing behind and making them beg from other people." This shows how much he cared for children and thought about their welfare.

The Prophet ﷺ also cared for the children of unbelievers. Whenever he went to the unbelievers to give them the message of Allah, they would be very rude and cruel to him. They inflicted different kinds of torture on him, but he never cursed the unbelievers.

Once while giving a talk, these unbelievers hurt him so badly that the Prophet ﷺ became unconcious. Even after this pain and sadness he still asked Allah to guide them to Islam.

Someone said, "O Prophet, please curse the unbelievers." The Prophet ﷺ replied, "Why should I pray for Allah to destroy them if they do not have faith in Allah? I hope that their children after them will one day believe in Allah."

This great kindness and forgiveness was because the Prophet was for all mankind. A curse on the unbelievers would bring great ruin on their children and the Prophet ﷺ did not want that.

Whether the children were orphans of unbelievers or Muslims, of friends or enemies, or had parents who were rich or poor, girls or boys, the Prophet ﷺ was merciful and kind to them all.

The Prophet ﷺ and the Arab Girls

The little girls of Arabia loved and respected the Prophet ﷺ dearly. He was sometimes even more dear to them than their own fathers. That was because the Prophet ﷺ loved them, cared for them and respected them. Unfortunately, some fathers did not want to have daughters and when they found out that a little girl had been born to them, they would be very sad and would even bury them alive. The Prophet ﷺ told all Muslims that this was very wrong and that all children, girls and boys, were blessings from Allah. The Prophet ﷺ took big sacrifices from fathers who had killed their daughters before Islam. He gave their camels in charity.

The Prophet ﷺ adored and loved his own daughter Fatima. When she grew up, he gave her so much respect. Whenever she came into the room, the Prophet ﷺ would spread a clean sheet on the floor for her to sit on. He loved Fatima's children so much, he would carry them on his shoulders. Sometimes when he prayed, his grandson would climb on his back and ride like a horse.

He loved and respected all the girls and boys of Islam as if they were his own. That is why whenever the Prophet ﷺ would pass by some place, girls would make up verses and sing his praises. In this way they were thanking their defender and helper. They mentioned the blessings he had bestowed on them. Sometimes they went too far in their praises for him and sang words which were not right. The Prophet ﷺ would stop them from singing these words.

Once the Prophet ﷺ attended a wedding ceremony where little girls were singing songs. The songs were in praise of their fathers and grandfathers. They were also praising the Prophet ﷺ. One of these songs was about how the Prophet ﷺ could tell what was going to happen tomorrow. As soon as the Prophet ﷺ learned about the words of this song, he stopped the girls from singing these words and told them to sing what they were singing before. When the girls heard this they took the words out of the song because they respected him and loved him.

The Prophet ﷺ always respected girls and asked the Muslims to love and respect them also.

The Theft of the Grapes

When Ibad's mother was dying, she had said to her son, "Son, when you grow up, I want you to go to Madinah and learn more about Islam."

Now Ibad was an orphan. He used to live on the outskirts of Madinah and was a shepherd of goats for a Jew. The Jew was very strict with him. He made him work hard and gave him very little to eat.

One day, the Jew was very angry about some little offence that Ibad had done, so Ibad ran away. Soon, he reached Madinah. He had been hungry since morning. He stopped near a garden. It was very cool near the stream where the grapevines were. He started to feel very hungry indeed. Ibad gazed at a bunch of grapes and thought, "If I take a few bunches of grapes I do not think that it will harm the garden." But then he realised that he would be stealing so he got up to leave.

Suddenly, a bunch of grapes knocked against his head

and started swinging. Ibad stopped and started to gaze at the bunch. His mouth opened and he started to suck the grapes. The sweet juice poured down his throat. Ibad could not help himself. Pressing the grapes with his two hands he started drinking the flowing juice. As he did so, he began to feel stronger and fresher.

He broke off some more bunches and hid them in his shirt and carried on walking. Just at that moment, someone who was standing behind a tree caught him by the neck. Some more boys also came running. The owner of the garden had caught him with the stolen grapes. Soon a crowd gathered there. In the midst of them, poor Ibad was in a terrible state. The only answer he could give to all their questions was, "Yes, I stole the grapes because I was hungry and thirsty." One youth was eager to hit Ibad but an older boy stopped him, saying, "You have no right to hit him. The decision of what to do lies with the Prophet ﷺ."

When the people were taking him to the Prophet ﷺ, poor Ibad was feeling very sorry for himself - not because of the fear of punishment, but because he did not want to face the Prophet ﷺ as a thief. This made him cry. He implored to the people, "You can give me whatever punishment you want. You can even cut off my head. But please do not take me to the Prophet ﷺ." The people said that they could not do that.

Dragging him along, they reached the Prophet ﷺ and told him the whole story. They told him how the boy had stolen the bunch of grapes. The Prophet ﷺ looked at the boy. Ibad told the Prophet ﷺ how he had reached Madinah. He told him how hunger had forced him to take the grapes, saying, "O Messenger of Allah, I swear by Allah that if I was not hungry I would never have touched the grapes."

The Prophet of mercy ﷺ looked at him for a few moments. Ibad trembled at the thought of his anger. Perhaps he thought in his heart, "May he give me as much punishment as he wishes, but I hope he will not be angry with me." Ibad stood with his head lowered.

Then he heard the Prophet's ﷺ voice. Ibad looked surprised and astonished at what the Prophet ﷺ was saying. He was telling the people, "He was unaware and you did not teach him. He was hungry and you did not feed him."

Ibad clasped the hands of the Prophet ﷺ. He was crying and said, "Thanks be to Allah that you are not angry with me."

The owner of the garden felt responsible for this. He felt that it was his fault that Ibad had stayed hungry and been forced to steal.

He asked the Prophet ﷺ whether Ibad could stay with him. He said he would take care of Ibad's food, clothing and education. So the Prophet ﷺ handed Ibad over to the owner of the garden.

The people of his time always consulted the Prophet ﷺ in such matters as he was a fair and just man.

Knowledge is Wealth

One day the Prophet ﷺ came out of his room and entered into the mosque of Madinah. People were doing different things - some were performing Salah, some were simply remembering Allah while others were sitting in an area called the Suffah, where they would study together. This was the first ever school in Islam. As the Prophet ﷺ entered the mosque all eyes turned towards him.

He walked into the mosque purposefully. Everyone wished that the Prophet ﷺ would sit beside him. The Prophet ﷺ looked around smiling and, to everyone's astonishment, he sat down among the students in the Suffah. He said, "Allah has sent me as a teacher." That is why he sat down where knowledge was being taught.

Allah has said that those who have faith will be given knowledge. If they continue to learn they will prosper. That is why our Prophet used to remind us that we should continue to learn.

Men, women and children are all supposed to seek knowledge. We must work hard to find knowledge no matter how far we have to go. To gain knowledge, we must overcome difficulties. We should gain knowledge in any way that we can."

Once the Prophet ﷺ asked 'Aisha ﷺ to learn to read and write. She was a very young girl but she listened to the Prophet ﷺ and learned. When he found out, he was very pleased.

The Prophet ﷺ used to care a lot for knowledge and learning. In the Battle of Badr, the Muslims captured many of the enemy. Some of them did not have enough money to buy their freedom but they could read and write. The Prophet ﷺ told them that they could earn their freedom by teaching Muslims how to read and write.

The Prophet ﷺ respected students very much. That is why he looked after the students of the Suffah. Often he would give food to them even though he may be hungry himself.

Once the Prophet ﷺ was sitting in the mosque of Madinah. Many people were crowded there. He was telling them about Allah and the way of Islam, when three men arrived. They saw the crowd. Two men came forward but the third man turned away. One of the two men found a place to sit where he could hear. He listened intently to what the Prophet ﷺ was saying. The other of the two men sat a little further away and did not try to come any nearer. He could not hear everything that the Prophet ﷺ was saying.

When the Prophet ﷺ finished his teaching, he said, "Hear about these men who just came. One of them came for the sake of knowledge. His tried his best to listen and came as close as he could. Allah gave him a place near to me and increased his knowledge. The other one did not want to make the effort of listening. Allah did not give him a place near me. The man could not listen to me and he could not increase in knowledge. The third man was unfortunate. He turned away from hearing knowledge and so Allah too turned away from him."

The Khalifah and the Lamp

Umar ibn 'Abd al-Aziz was a great Khalifah from Bani Umayyah, a famous tribe of Makkah. When he was appointed Khalifah, he took all of his wife's jewellery and gave it to the Muslims. Some people from his tribe had land which they had taken illegally from the government. He took that land and gave it to the poor. He brought justice and mercy to the oppressed and the unfortunate who had been dealt with cruelly.

He took only two small silver coins called dirhams from the treasury to live on and so his life was very simple. Before he became Khalifah, he was known for living a splendid and luxurious life but now he was Khalifah, he lead a more simple life than most ordinary men.

Once a man came to see Khalifah Umar ﷺ and stayed with him for some time. While they were talking, the oil in the lamp finished and the lamp went out. Khalifah Umar's servant was sleeping nearby. The guest said, "Allow me to wake up your servant so that he can put oil in the lamp." Khalifah Umar ﷺ said, "There is no need to wake the servant." The guest asked, "Then may I fill it with oil?" Khalifah Umar ﷺ replied, "No, you are my guest. I do not ask my guests to work for me. I will light the lamp myself."

Then Khalifah Umar ﷺ got up, went and found the oil, put it in the lamp and finally lit it. Then he sat down next to his guest and said, "I was Umar when I got up and lit the lamp and I am still Umar. Doing this little task does not lower a man's dignity."

Khalifah Umar ﷺ was a very humble man and never asked anyone to do anything for him if he could do it himself.

Uwais al-Qarni

There lived many great and noble men and women at the time of the Prophet ﷺ. This is the story of one such noble man called Uwais. Uwais lived in Najd and his tribe were called Qaran.

He lived at the time of the Prophet ﷺ but he never met him although he always wanted to. The reason for that was because he had a very old blind mother. She had no one beside her son to look after her and care for her. Uwais was a shepherd and he raised camels for a living.

Whenever he made up his mind to go and meet the Prophet ﷺ, he would think of his mother and realise that it was more important that he look after her.

Uwais loved the Prophet ﷺ very much. During the battle of Uhud, he heard that the Prophet ﷺ had lost some teeth and so he broke the same teeth in his own mouth.

The Prophet ﷺ knew about Uwais and his love for him

and so the Prophet ﷺ loved and respected Uwais, too.

One day, the Prophet told two of his Companions, Umar Faruq ☙ and Ali ☙, to give some of his clothes to Uwais after he died. He also told them to ask Uwais to pray for the Muslims.

When the Prophet ﷺ passed away, Umar ☙ and Ali ☙ went to Uwais to give him the clothes of the Prophet. Uwais cried in grief. When he stopped crying, Umar ☙ asked Uwais to pray for the Muslims just as the Prophet ﷺ had asked.

Uwais prayed for the blessings of Allah on the Muslims and Allah accepted his prayer. It is said that, "The Muslims will expand to be as many as the hairs on the goats of the tribes of Rabiah and Hizar." No other tribes in Arabia had as many goats as these two tribes did. Now try to imagine all the hairs on all the goats that they had.

Some people say that Allah gave this special blessing to Uwais because he cared for his mother. He was so close to Allah that the Prophet ﷺ told Umar ☙ and Ali ☙ to ask him to pray for the Muslims.

His love for the Prophet ﷺ was so great that even though he never met him he has been given the status of a Companion of the Prophet.

We must also look after our mothers and we must love and respect the Prophet ﷺ and the best way to do this now that he is no longer with us is to follow his example.